WEBSONGS

ONORUOIZA MARK ONUCHI

WEBSONGS

ONORUOIZA MARK ONUCHI

WEBSONGS
ONORUOIZA MARK ONUCHI

ISBN 978-978-790-678-1

SKILL CREST MEDIA IMPRINT
+2348032321886
skillcrestmedia007@gmail.com

Dedication

Dedicated to God,

The Superlative Muse

Whose poetic craft,

colourful verses and compelling

notes

Ignite my wakeful thoughts

and trigger my latent dreams!

ACKNOWLEDGEMENTS

My heartfelt appreciation goes to Uzor Maxim Uzoatu, the Boroja warhead who amiably agreed to read and comment on the first draft, gracias!

Many thanks to Ofuma Agali, my literary chief of over a decade and counting for reading the final draft with deep insight and clinical direction.

Special thanks to Uche Uwadinachi, my Poet laureate who pushed me beyond my limits to make this happen; Abraham Obakachi, for his insistent prodding, holistic critique and outstanding input; Professors Olu Obafemi and Charles Bodunde, my eminent connoisseurs cum revolutionary lecturers who took me on a timeless sail across literary climes and lexical shuttles of literary pantheons; Filza Chaudhry of the iconic tribe of bohemian wordsmiths for her remarks and intellectual engagement;

Big thanks to my siblings for their support: Victoria Olagunju, Vivian Agboola, Ben Onuchi, Peter Onuchi and Vero Dan-Ikpoyi and my beloved mum, Mary Onuchi.

Special thanks to my wife, Adetutu Onuchi-Mark for being my number one cheerleader and vibrant support, you are cherished!

To many others who have supported me on this journey, I say thank you!

Some of the poems have appeared in The Guardian Life, ThisDay, National Interest, Crossroads (an anthology of Poetry for Okigbo) amongst others. Some were also featured in online platforms, this has helped as a feedback loop to feel the pulse of readers.

CONTENTS

PREFACE

As a lexical nomad, beyond an expeditioner; crafting timeless pieces of art affirms one's irrefutable commitment as a crusader of words to speak truth to power for humanity to underscore. It's been a tapestry of a congenial kind: lacing lexical typescripts for radical engagements across borders.

I salute my tribesmen, griots and antinormians who waft melodies of maladies and craft royal rhythms of pristine harmony; turning heavy mounds of hate into mountains of hallowed tomes. These works captured my Odyssey of over a decade, as a journeyman whose endless romance with tomes required an outlet of some kind, I endlessly nursed this dream.

This hybrid meshed over the years is a reflection of the resilience of a lingering mission which metamorphosed into a web of varied narratives intersected by a horde of voices: raw, royal, resilient, angry, hopeful, invigorating, passionate, wild, boisterous and manacled with elliptical smears.

The collection metaphorically criss-crosses the dale of pedestrian dungeons to the hill of hallowed mansions with a spotlight on Nigeria, Africa and then the world: a pontification of humanity as globalised reality in the most plebeian form.

The expression of humanity in every syllable is an affirmation of our values, faith and persuasions beyond colour, creed and country!

- Onoruoiza Mark ONUCHI

Flakes of Pain

YOUR IMPERIAL MAJESTY

Your feeble hymn rings!
couched in the maggots
of sickened kites that roam our skies
of rust-buckets that navigate our coasts
of our death-trap lanes
wolfing lives behind wheels at will.
Of hunger pangs that roam our hapless belly
of erratic lights that blurs and blinks
of the waning naira whose valueless droop
has famished the hood
of tax barons fattened by tottered tax payers
drained and puttered.
Of poverty strutting with glee on our streets
welcome to the planet's poverty hotbed!
Of constant hijacks by Fulani herdsmen
of kidnaps that regularly blight the dreams of waning men
of endless floods rippling lives with drowning pellets
of disarray in the corridors of clout
of callous pawns spilling with rage innocent pullets!
It is yet another term your majesty!
You have fed us with the chaffs of illusion
clothed us with garments of penury
you have ostracized our eggheads
and replaced them with dunderheads
our economy bleeds with pain of terror
our wages have failed to pull our paling weights
our land mourns and grieves over the death of many
of our blooming gold
that now spell doom before our very eyes!
Your majesty the list is endless.
We desperately await
the next level of change you pledged...

WHY?

Why will you crown clowns in a turf of topnotch prodigies?

To waffle banal rhythms in the face of colossal chaos?

Why will you enthrone a loony king amidst a phalanx of civil patriots?

To ruin the kingdom and ridicule the sacred throne?

Why will you leave a drunk behind the wheel of change?

To ram you into the lagoon of lunatics and a vale of skulls?

Why will you arm a blind tramp to man the entrance of your mansion?

To be pummelled by tyrants from Hell and your abode reduced to rubbles?

Why will you embrace a Delilah and entrust your life into her hands?

To waste your wealth, wane your strength and finally hurl you into Hades?

Why will you dine with the devil and wine with its mistress?

To wake up in hell and wallow in eternal misery?

Why, I ask?

I ask why?

STOCKLESS HAY

(To all institutions of learning in chaos)

Crumbling walls in stubble of ruin

pervade academic towers

like the charred remains of Hiroshima after Tibbets' invasion

relics of a once vibrant culture reek with grief

now intellectual apostates and batty drones

have inherited once chaste lecterns

where they reel void shells devoid of yolk

wafting illusions into strings of corruption

in ramshackle ivory domes

to infantile folks with bloated bellies

stuffed with flakes of rust

their infertile realms of diluted tomes

eloquently affirm their shallow creation

emblazoned with brazen mediocrity

as they dance to flagon's command

and eve's seductive request

no!

Not in the times of yore

when eggheads once trod with impeccable grace

as custodians of knowledge

crafting well-honed ideas on our artless boards

arbiters in the game of intellectual wit

once trudged through this wilderness

with golden plumes and prized medallion of conquest

couched with lofty letters

now exiled by dictators and their goons

our valiant pantheons hanker for safety in safer shores

swelling brain-gain in foreign zones

while our territory is punctured into stagflation

like the bulging ribs of a hapless guttersnipe

I weep for my land and its institutions

confined to the abyss by a bunch of mindless gladiators

I mourn…

I wail…

ON THE BRINK

The claws of darkness
polluted skies
on sting rage
meshed with patches of fury
cyclically embroiling a pariah nation
of doomed vales and vile frames
twilight culture in motion
frenetically wrestling with a 19th Century invention
light, light and light in extinction
obscurity, Nigeria's middle name
pervaded by a murky romance with endless monsters
from topline chambers to downtown dingy
clamped in nightfall at dawn
and grey gawks
in shadows of gloom
with scars of agony
of despots in mortal dance
a daze in a maze
of hemlocks and preys
a muddle of blistered scars…
rippling feeble mist
gory story
hazy tides
trailing deaths
lethal lore
vanity is your serenity
with orgy rhythms
glowing embers of devastation
in sanity famished skyline
looming echoes swing
vermillion shades
of flatulent epic
blurred masks
despots on constant sails…
welcome to the nocturnal mash of Africa…

BRAZEN RECESSION

Economic crunch crushing climes
collapsing castles
creating gorges of confusion
of claps of thunder crumbling skyscrapers
in high profile business districts
of financial implosion and poverty explosion
piercing hearts with chronic convulsion
from Australia to Venezuela the rhythm rings
clipping off wings of wealth
crippling corporations with glee
crashing domes
from the Atlantic to the Mediterranean
cropping cords to delusion
a clampdown on money makers
clenching its fist of fire and ravaging homes with want
your crafty clout rubbished the graft of conmen's shrewd
manipulations
then we heard enough of your crunchy conversations
your phantom wheel and ghostly glide
have left smart kids on their knees
enough of your hazy steam
on our sheds and shelters!
enough!
Hercules must salvage this Augean stable
pervaded by cronies of disorder
to entrench a cloudburst
that will usher in the long awaited windfall...

VILE SHEPHERDS

*(For sham Prophets that parade vain temples & phoney worship
centres)*

The dome of worship
reeks with profane songs dedicated to mammon
here lecherous priests arrayed in lordly cassock
pollute vestal altars
with tainted garments of randy escapades
seeing phoney visions and rehearsed revelations
a leech to the artless congregation
they turned the once revered vestry
into a chamber of fetish libations
riddled with carrions and maggots
for the prodigal rabbi now waft diluted sermons
a divine calling perforated by ephemeral passion
for their antics in the sacred temple
emits smokes of rebellion
making artless worshippers twice the children of hell
they plundered hallowed altars
and turned chaste castles to harems of babel
their cruel clout and sacrilegious stride
shall be denuded by the Omniscient!
And the time appointed draws near...

FLICKERS

The raging spill

of bottled flames

with implosive guile

rattles the subtle manoeuvre

of a deified overlord

rankling men under the coop of steel

whittling scams of scum

a drivel –

of mashed bait of doom

as many squeal and scowl...

Welcome to the republic of despots

where fiery storms of hunger honks
at will

and traps on tracks guzzle lives

with deafening chills!

Drained hopes
shall soon be revived

By passionate tramps

On the road to redemption -

we fight!

FAILING VAULTS

Grey groans...

Livid moans...

On bad loans

GLOOMY GALE

Flapping wings of triumph

through rigid clouds and darkened galaxies

where raging infernos stir the bowel of the ethereal

it is our desire to float with gusto

across the ashes of pain

we have had enough of the searing talons of the vulture

we have had enough of the tumultuous quakes

that gulped innocent victims

we have had enough of the political turmoil

that claimed lives and maimed hearts

we have had enough of economic crisis

that clogged hoods and hauled hagglers

we have had enough...

Desolate
Drums

DUST TO DUST

Infant born
noble bred
regal robes
life of boon
in mansions and castles
across seas and beyond shores
but twilight echo
invades with vermillion claws
dust to dust...
A genius born
nurtured with a barrage of tomes
on learned hoods
with a bunch of scrolls
a prolific pantheon
from towers of esteem
loaded with brain and brawn
hacked at midlife by scavengers of doom
now buried into the loins of the earth
six feet deep
dust to dust...
A restless kid in rags of grey
cackling away
in a hovel somewhere in a battered slum
where hunger leaps and poverty struts
he hobbles with a bloated belly
sockets gone hollow
by daily struggles with tons of need
the curtain finally falls
picture fades
as he heeds the summons of the midnight call
dust to dust...
Whether pale or plump
black or blonde
green or grey
haggard or hulky
bleak or bright
gaunt or groomed
to dust shall all return
dust to dust...

TRANSMIGRATION

(For Femi Aluko, a prized ally who was cornered by the cold claws of a
delusive imp)

Mourning this morning ...
Ululation rents the famished air
of a saintly soul snatched
by the talons of an ominous wind
why have you left your buddy in this cold hapless night?
why must the raging sea
swallow your vestal being of lofty creation?
in an arid haven of banal constipation
you were my Fidus Achates
who shattered my lonesome shell
with your magic gait of bubbling zest
I still see your winsome grandeur
in dark and dreary nights
your resplendent gaze
a treasured boon in a haven of heartless tramps
I remember the banters, the pleasantries
that trailed our shelter
with glee in a wilderness void of love
 cluttered with rust and lust
only to be de-lived by the drooling fangs
of our immortal prey
why must you at the very prime of creative vivacity
succumb to the cruel beckon of a callous foe
gobbled by the pangs of hades
just at the threshold of triumph
you were snatched by that illusive tyrant!
Oh femi!
Knocked down by the ill-wind of severe pains
the pains and troubles are now over
as you enjoy the splendour of eternal clime
continue to rest under his everlasting wings of lofty habitation
until inevitability and us
merge again with the heavenly throng!!

MAYHEM CITY (For Jos, a city in ruins)

Rising inferno…
Pungent smokes choking space with glee
cadavers, burnt cars and trucks litter the lanes...
Ignited by myopic militants
in search of vermillion scars
the earth boils with unflinching rage
from the hazy lairs of cruel urchins
to the modest abodes of artless hearts…
Once a serene city now bleeds with brazen uprising!
Rupturing the communal bond
that once pervaded the orb

Jos!
Once a beehive of ebullient folks
a tin city of radiant sun
where virgin flakes rumbled from the foggy sky.

Let this raging tussle end
let this persistent hatred cease
sheathe your swords of war
and mend those broken walls
let's fight this lingering flaw!

Peace we plead
peace is all we need
peace… peace!

PROGRESSION

Here we are - a world of pilgrims

on an endless sojourn

from the spring of innocence

dancing merrily to life's constant mutations

the summer of sunshine gradually sets in

bubbling radiantly in the prime of vigour

hinged in the brink of endless permutations

tangled with twists and turns

time steadily glides to midlife

of mixed colours of autumn

like a fleeting phase winter suddenly encroaches

to herald a nightfall of waning strength

fading hairs and head

tilting towards midnight

and then life finally fades out...

SILENT WHISPER

Your escapades echo around my earlobes

as the arrowhead of a randy carnival

shooting arrows of cupid at maidens

to satiate your erotic clout

your fiery phallus invading territories of variant norms

you have slaughtered victims in their multitude

leaving them with the whispering silence of a phantom

a monster with the genteel gait of a lamb

your phoney garb emblazoned with a shade of red and white

reeks with hate the deeds of a churlish reveller

but wait…

From green to grey

from gangly to chubby

have you consumed

your grave you have dug with your scaly hands

as justice now haunts your dreams

and nemesis stalks your hope

your life in shards evidently speaks

of the gruelling grip of death's trailing hold

judgment is here!

COFFERS DRAINERS

The smiling faces and dazzling eyes tell
of a gathering far from unpleasant yell
for the celebration by a chieftain
in the echelon of monetary fountain
as he joins the billionaire league
nobody cares if he is the coffers rogue
whose mission in the lofty house of boom
leaves the talakawas in a famished state of doom
for here in his palatial dome
like a monumental cathedral in Rome
lives he in a regal style of bliss
a lion in the jungle roaming with ease
where he lavishes without haste
mouth-watering meals of great taste
where many are left to starve to death
and thrown unburried to the harried earth
outside his glistening portals
giving no value to famished mortals
a cosmos of unequals in a battle
like the battle between the rat and cattle
cause my wailing heart to bleed
if only we throw off our corrupt garment to wisdom heed
then shall our world experience a harmonious order
void of chaotic and ceaseless murders

Vestiges of Hope

SCRIPTED LINES

I have heard songs

from various tongues

I have heard hymns

of various themes

I have heard rhymes

at various times

I have ranted lines

through novel climes.

I have had lyrical glimpse

beyond the physical realm of natural beams

pleasant songs void of gongs

have touched my soul making me right my wrong

echoes of their warmth

have worked wonders

in my dark moments of wrath

melodic songs have soothed my pains

and tamed my rage

soothing balms of crafted chants

have healed wounds

and those once bound

by chains and pains

releasing tears of hope

like the waterfall from the virgin sky

through the hills to the vale

have enlivened my scorching earth

let the songs and hymns resound!

ON THE VERGE

I have wrestled with titanic tomes
and cruel gnomes
flinging jabs in restless bouts
to conquer the brazen illusion
that relentlessly stalks my dream
of a callous phantom that drains my rain
leaving on its trail
a melody of maladies
feet of fetters
and a flood of blood
to sway me off the rail
to the sidewalk of mediocrity
where the loony goons of barbaric barons reside
while the political hawks of gluttonous glee dominate the dome
to short-change my toil with a barrage of adversities.

I will elope with hope
to a new realm of possibilities
where I long for an unsullied song
that will bring the spring of idyllic realm
there I will learn, relearn and unlearn
I will master the art of combat in the woods
like David, I shall return as a man of valour
to reclaim this lost paradise from the abyss of hell!

HUSTLE

The city bustles
and struggle rules
here life is drenched in the inferno
of endless spin
with restless souls scampering for survival
and idle hearts gnawed by starvation's cruel claws
it is awake with promises of paradise
for those who hustle
from the wake of dawn to the nap of dusk
for those who wrestle with the shadows of night
will be haunted by the nemesis of their deeds
while the proselytes and their acolytes pervade the scene
with sermons from the mount
of various divides
the swinging vibes from babel
will ceaselessly haunt vain vagrants
carousing with the daughters of eve
the unfolding drama of life
is embedded in the hassle for survival
in this edgy jungle
where constant rumble
is the name of the game:
soar or crumble!

CROSSROADS

Spawning web of choices
and babel of clatters
strive hard to captivate your glances
in this dense orb of perpetual perplexity
where vain hushes, blank whispers and husky screams of complexity
conspire to swirl you off course...
leaving behind the consequences of walking a flawed trail
and a distorted vision primed to fail
with an aftertaste of a sore tongue
and the ultimate foghorn
of foiled destinies
crushed dreams and aspirations...
As we walk through this dark vale
of no easy sail
we will clutch to him
who knows the perfect choice
that'll alter our lives for good...

NIGHT

I am the night that beclouds your horizon
… the might to stunt your calculated moves at dawn
I caught you searching for the hidden pearls under the arid soil
beyond the coast of travail
I capture your dogged moves to conquer your world
as you diligently traverse this caste
I, the night, will blur your vision
… foil your mission by my clout of treachery
…trail your steps
and hound your footfalls to delusion
I will wane your strength
clutter your path with traps of pain
you shall not have that coveted gold of radiance
but amidst these darts hurled at you from my fortress
I still see you rising meticulously
from that debris of shattered vases
from the dunghill of lonesome torture
you have shoved relenting to the edges!
I will plague your day with burdens
that drain the strength of men
I will scorch you with the sun of frustration!
but like the gyrfalcon
you have swallowed up beating like a harmless pill
by these convoluted maze of persecution
what?
Like the eagle you have soared high!
high above the sky
beyond the reach of my fetters
beyond my domain have you flown
to declare judgment.
Now you leave me in chains.

GLIDE

The misty cloud crawls

through blurred binoculars

of grey tramps on refuge-voids

in an orb of castles and palaces

where effigies inhabit cottage of royalty.

Gluttonous harvesters embark on vain hounds

of artless hustlers on tedious shuttles

dawn is green

dusk is grey.

This eternal transition

will herald hope

to the oppressed perpetual pangs

that ceaselessly stalks their virgin dreams

for this domain shall restore to them

the bliss of paradise

and the violators of the earthy rule

shall be tossed into an endless realm of pain.

NATIONAL MALAISE

The moist from the cloudy mist
engulfs with horror our nascent breath
we want and wane in endless spree
yawning and yearning for a hustler's dime
the widening chasm envelops our orb
where the masses must till and toil
for a frugal loaf to salvage their hollow belly
while our political drones feed fat with glee
on our national coffers meant for us all
they have plundered our wealth with impunity
igniting the embers of disunity!
the persistent cry of our collective pain
Shall send them to where they belong...
For Karma's rod shall surely descend on erring perforators
I see a new order...
Void of brazen chaos and executive larceny

Threshold of Triumph

HEROIC WELCOME

The earth wakes with a morning mist
 roaring with a burst of resplendent feast
I feel the supple rhythm pulsating through ecstatic hearts
timeless spin of radiant vistas engulf our horizon
we are on the threshold of change
as we assemble fractured eggshells of life's evolving symphony
sharpshooters have we become firing from an accurate range
dispelling with glee all that play the loony phony
we are on the crest of redemption
where eagles of skilful flight gather to take strategic action
as we soar to lofty heights
and unravel unfathomable depths
through gleaming seams and flaming rays
our starry crowns and stellar thrones await our gladiatorial welcome!
Welcome aboard!

THORNY CREST

On the crest
crafting rhymes with fibres of timeless test
honing my latent skill
and sharpening my beak for a constant kill
I must dine with the Muse
to savour a relishing lexical fuse
the Argus presides here
here I must knowledge share
in this Rocky Mount
where you must exercise energy of endless count.
I'm on the threshold of re-invention
like the phoenix on the verge of transformation
to experience an invigorating birth
that will herald a rebirth
I'm here to see the eagle roam the skies
with steely talons and penetrative eyes
I'm here to polish my claws against predators
from overblown liquidators that drain our wealth
leaving our economy with paralysed feet.
I'm here in this idyllic ambience
to enjoy the chaste bloom of nature's essence
to converse with the moon at dusk
and merry with the earthlings at nature's hilly tusk
as I incubate inventive fabrics from this misty terrain
I feel the abundance of rain
that will herald an unprecedented boon!
Feel free, it's still noon…

FLAMING LIGHT

Light up your hazy night

for a galvanic flight

with a calculated might

and a keen insight

to take a ground-breaking flight

and conquer unfathomable heights

to a paradise of inexplicable sight

we will share our stories bright

from the furnace that breeds our ultimate right

ushering us into a new world of dazzling light

A DREAMER'S PARADISE

I once calmed a torrid cloud

built a castle upon its sphere

and rolled down the moon as my royal carpet

my imaginative power ran wild

I invented mansions of exotic architectural designs

sublime wing-boats, yachts and automobiles

flooded my realm

with golden walls round about my domain

and infested my castle with pearls from Eden

I banished evil from my territory and enthroned peace and wisdom

I guaranteed all day of bliss and no night of pain

with ease, perfect governance was restored

upon a domain that was once ruined by pain and delusion

and all enjoyed the paradise of unending merriment...

TRANSITION

Moon beams
boon dreams
sunny trails after a rainstorm
from the pellets of the hallowed clouds
with steely flakes of restless bites
now the terrestrial plains bask
in the domain of radiant healing
from the rays of an energetic burst
it screams with resplendence...
restoration beckons!

MY ART
I do not fart for art
it runs through the depths of the heart
I have mastered the craft
beyond the game of raft
and the pontification of a daft
life is art
void of vain dart
not an empty cart
art is life
for all to thrive
be art
fight for humanised art...

PEARLY SEARCH

Don't roam the night

in search of dawn

don't walk the path of corruption

in search of integrity

don't dine with fools in search of wisdom

the reality of productive practicality

is webbed on the lane of sanity

where knowledge rules

and wisdom reigns

for drunks and rogues rule at night

but men of candour and insight patronise light

while sharpshooters take flight

wingless laggards aimlessly fight

in a world of rapid development

where resounding intellect is a unique testament

to an enduring legacy of eternal value

CONSCRIPTED SERVITUDE

Conscripted to serve her fatherland
hurled into the interior of a jungle
to bring succour to indigent wastrels
whose lifeline is entrenched in the harried earth
to mould heavy mounds of humus heaps
to salvage famished kindred from the claws of starvation.

I was conscripted to serve in an alien land
far from modern invention
to join the train backwoods men
to hack the path to civilization
to crush ancient dogmas to extinction.

I was conscripted to serve
to bring to their domain the good tidings of democracy
to banish the callous hold of illiteracy
to translate the jungle peasants to men and women of distinction
to bridge the divide of ethnic bickering through dialogic confrontations
to propagate the gospel of peace
to the erring wastrels of pervasion
to implant on young minds the essence of education
to serve as a beacon in a hazy enclave

Yes!
Conscripted to transform men of stygian disposition
to men of radiant illumination
to teach them modernity
through intellectual clinics of translation
to mould fragmented souls
into harmonious wholes
conscripted to serve!
to illuminate darkened paths
to leave indelible foot walks in the sand of time
for subsequent highfliers
to reap with multiple harvests in due time

(Dedicated to sylvan National Youth Service Corps Members, the past,
the present and the future)

INVADERS
(For my famished fatherland deflated by imperial lords)

Sunk in a twilight reverie
dilating binoculars skyward
beholding nature's awesome wonders
as the galaxy of stars radiated our ambience
illuminating the moonlight tales
sequestered in the backwoods of bliss
savouring and sheltering round the night fire
with random gales we heard
griot songs of ancient myths
woven round gnomes and legendary figures
we constantly giggled with glee
and danced to the rhythms of the whistling wind
it was all a delightful conference
void of vitiate vampires but....
But the long drawn tale suddenly fragmented
with vermillion stars speckled with rage
cluttered with murky songs of hate
as the pale blue sky
constantly beclouded our horizon
with hooting owls heralding foghorns of danger
suddenly...
Suddenly sterile impostors of racial blond
invaded our Edenic territory
parading their garbs as ambassadors of peace
but have now plundered our pristine gourd
they have manacled our venerated custodians
clobbered their conscience and gagged their visions
and now we hear dirges
cascading from the hollow drums
of a once vibrant culture with her ethos
diluted by the callous creed
of a bestial race
when shall we sing again Uhuru songs?
Void of patches of modernity
to return to the cradle of our blissful haven

DAWN

Nature's charm Unveiled at dawn
the aesthetics of universal artistry
a reflection of exotic elegance...
Architectural divinity
forged with the craftsmanship Of the Sublime...

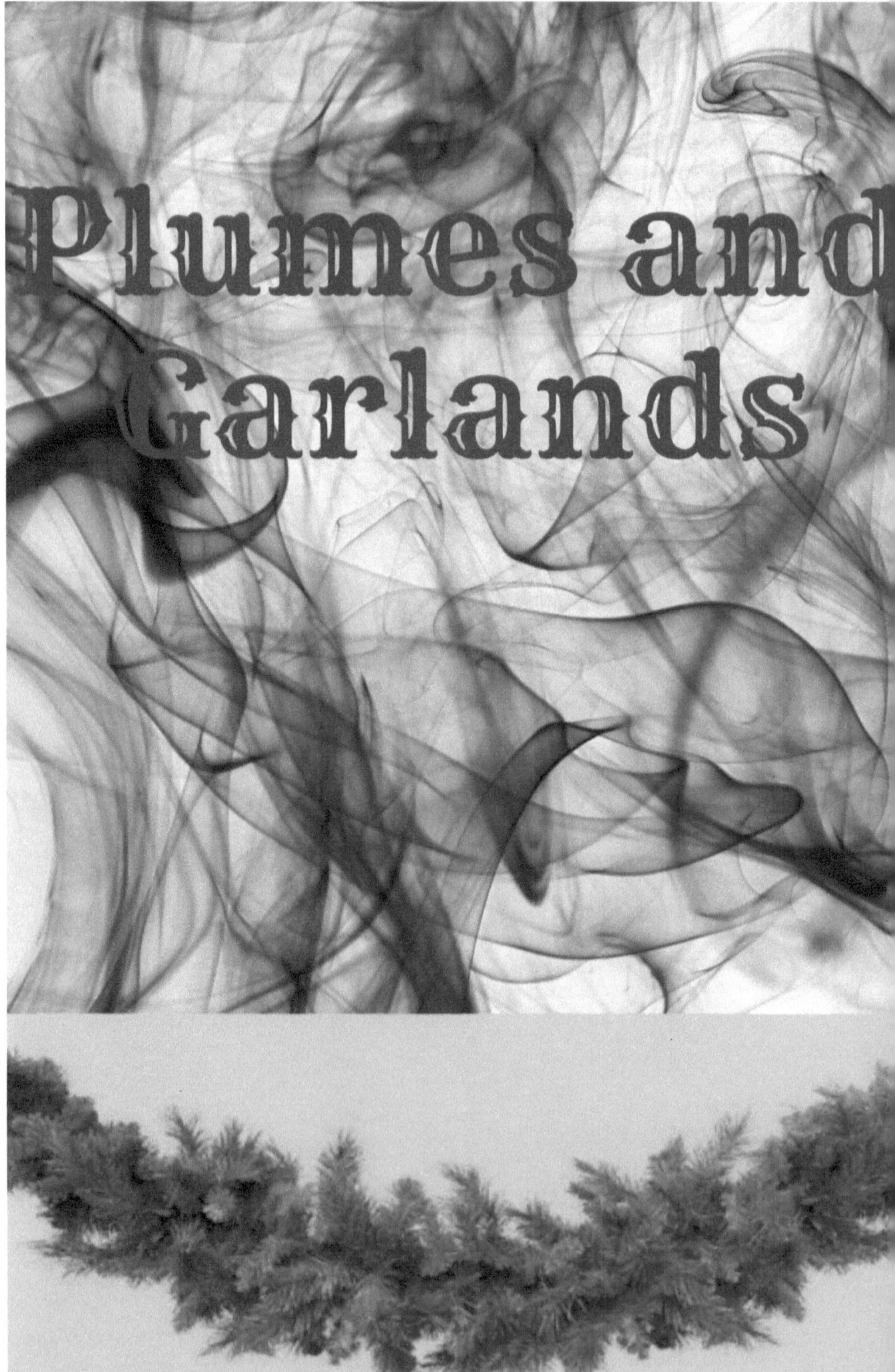

Plumes and Garlands

LET'S CELEBRATE   (For Professor Charles Bodunde)

Babbles of Babel!
from inept folks of their ilk
quaking with fueled flames
of greenhorns scribbling shaggy lines disjointedly bland
cluttered with vague and equivocal direction;
in clusters of confusion!
Crude as ancient routes to deserted hamlets
but the cerebral navigator burnished with literary gemstones
ushered our panting hearts
into the flawless spring of creativity
his artful verses crafted with piquant panache
lingered in our infantile minds!
We brought our slack and dreary lines with feeble textures
before our revered pantheon
who honed our skills in the creative canvas of refinement
and rekindled our passionate flames of lingering tunes
on the dunes of connubial climes!
He took us through the classical school of prominent bards
to the postmodernist construct of complex griots
we have eaten literary rusks
from the cauldron of our prolific scholar
whose words woven in the loom of radiant colours
provoke enchanting notes of delightsome ardour!
your lyrical chants purl through our ecstatic hearts;
for you taught us how to make fertile mounds in an arid orb.
We have indeed dined with the muse!
for we have drank from your nectar pot
and the honeyed taste provoked us to ask for more!
Let our goblets click;
let our mouths dance to the prodding of gateau!
Let's cavort the stage with merriment!
For we know that more laurels will follow!
as we celebrate your valiant conquest
in this terrain of arbiters!

MAN OF THE MOMENT
(For Dr. Akintoye Akindele)

His cerebral stride of iconic glide
reflects the unflinching passion
of an arrowhead on a ground-breaking sail.
Empowering lives
changing tides
standing apart in miles
with unalloyed thirst for more.
He remains the crowned king
of continental business
a decorated philanthropist on a gallant voyage
with trophies, laurels and garlands to affirm…
The man in the spotlight!
Swamped by investors, technocrats,
entrepreneurs, scholars and orphans
he is in your neighbourhood
like Santa to make your dreams come through.
A validator of visions
a pathfinder of distinction
connecting the dots
to transform a sagging clan
from the backwoods of pain
to the frontline of bliss.
It's time to roll out the drums
for drumbeats of ease
as we join the throng
to celebrate the magical muse
who turns every business to gold
and spins every misery to bloom
to lift every failing enterprise
into a behemoth of boom
Africa is rising from the doldrums
to a new season of brightening floodlights
and bubbling grace.
Thank you,
Committed Crusader of revolutionary transformation
for rising to the demands of the season…

I AM...

(Dedicated to all skillful poets across climes and tongues)

The capacity of the word
is profound with power to confound
 as a lexical priest
and an oracle of the word
words roll with vigour
to dispel and compel erring gladiators.

Words are weapons of war
garnered with the deft skill of a commandant
whose ingenious craft sends adversaries to the dale of doom
words with lyrical flavour calm ailing hearts
bringing succour to agitated souls
words are spirits with incalculable influence
as a merchant of words
power to transform, perform and reform flow like the Nile

I am a word hustler
a lyrical scribe
a peddler of rhythms
meshing versified fibres with the ease of a seasoned craftsman
like the skillful goldsmith i refine crooked verses into royal rhymes
I have shaped words into searing swords
swords that have slain kings
and elevated slaves into stars
like the master baker i make and bake men with my twofold ballpoint
I bar and mar men with my dual arsenal
as an expressive sharpshooter, i have pulled down brazen walls of
droning thrones
and have enthroned industrious crowns
I am a valiant crusader of the word
I am a POET!

CONQUEST (For Christopher Okigbo, 1932-67)

We are still mourning
after several decades of waning
when bullets of pervasion
hurled from the fortress of fevered foes
ripped out your mortal temple
sending you on a sudden flight of transmutation.
We are still mourning
your sudden home call
for we remember with nostalgia
your legendary strides in lyrical chants
you were neither a voluble void
nor a laconic limper
but a prodigious word carver
hewing words with crystal craft
you were neither a muse in a maze
nor an insipid poetic panther
but a ducal griot that hounded
errant foxes from their lecherous lair
OKIGBO!
You were the moon that denuded
the murky escapades of twilight merchants
you were a proficient bard
that churned out pellets and missiles
on erring political pantheons
you wove graphic looms with potent fibres
striking cords with artistic vigour
you were indeed a flaming candle
in an arid night through your evocative poesy
though you vanished like the mayfly
at the threshold of productive harvest
your crafted submissions were not evanescent flakes at winter
but like the myrtle the fragrance lingers
your rustic gusto was a testament
to your connubial romance
with nature and culture
your legacy in letters of gold
crested in our minds lingers…

UNSUNG HEROES

(For all unsung heroes across the world)

The scars of your war-weary hands
the insignia of your toil-battered spine
in a world soiled by persistent toil
and an age smeared by constant war
leaving victims in dismal health
far from comfort and wealth
the echoes of ache
from the hinterlands, midlands to the main lands
across various divides
leave trails of distress
where inventions by artless men
are cornered by brazen cartels
with clout to swing rhythms
to their parlous domain
leaving the hero in tears of dispossession
the legacy of your heroic crusade
in a world of unsung heroes
shall be excavated for celebration
your generation shall reap from
where you have tirelessly sown
you shall recover all
from the villains that perpetuate their schemes
they shall face the wrath of their cunning hands
for justice delayed shall not be denied
to our unsung heroes:
tireless women, devoted mothers, dedicated fathers
war veterans, community leaders, unknown inventors...
dead or alive
the price of your toil
shall be paid in full...
To you...
To your generation...

TRAMPS ON TOMES

I once scurried through a jungle of tomes

in search of pearls and timeless treasures

I reeled through...

from the languid turf of hazy hagglers

to the esoteric sphere of cryptic connoisseurs

the jagged rhythm pulsating with a staccato of pebbles

not a placid clime but a wonky wilderness

where your eyes rove for honey of rising cadence

only to decelerate

from alien territories to corny sceneries

yet the quest to quench the irrepressible void lingers

the passion to conquer volatile shorelines

dense jungles and congenial streams persist

let the voyage of discovery continue...

For those who dare to soldier on

RAGING SAGE

Spilling rage

from the spleen of a scribbled page

the clout of the pen leaps

with a passionate current

that only a hurting heart can muster

the nifty scrawl booms louder than a city brawl.

This age of scribal levitation

ignites constant meditation

writers commune ...

politicians are not immune

to the missiles

that explosively flutter

from their inventive machinery.

This is the age of rage

the golden stage for the scripted page

the season for the resourceful sage

to swipe political hawks till they stagger

because the pen is mightier than a silver-plated dagger

the inflamed sage must wield his lexical pellets

for the rebirth he earnestly seeks

until his pain ceases...

WHAT IS POETRY?

It is scripted chants of esoteric verses
veiled with metaphors of illusion
caked in abstract polemics
to haunt artless binoculars.

What is poetry?
Lyrical ballads crafted with artistic candour
couched in lucid diction
for the rustic and the urbane
it is the symmetry of letters
configured with the twirl of inspiration
of the muse whose canine clout
echoes with rhymes of delight.

What is Poetry?
A complex corpus of syllabic mutation
stringed with skill like a weaver's web
by royal lords of words
seasoned bards of skillful vibes
and generic muse of royal birth.

What is poetry?
Poetry is...

WINGMAN

(For Dayo Phillips)

Your eagle roving eyes

Ignite the flame of unalloyed passion

your dexterity in the dynamics of penmanship

inflames my fingers to conjure intricate looms

you stand colossally tall in this enterprise

embroiled with unrivalled ingenuity

to brainstorm novel voyage of discovery

beaming flashlights into nocturnal corners

that harbour priceless pearls in this pristine landscape

your lynx binoculars

stands you tremendously towering above your peers

in the enterprise of words

brilliant craft of creativity.

Your noble quest with dogged consummation

blooms with boom

and the dividends shall

spread through distant climes and neighbouring zones

hallowed with the intellectual fervor of Marx

elegant oratory of Solon

ride on wordsmith

with your literary assegai!

the world feeds voraciously

on your compelling crusts..

Echoes of
Love

LOVE CASTLE

Come with me, my love...

To paradise

we have struggled with haunting shadows

stalked by raging storms

harassed by unending uproar

it is time to soar

join me as I take you to Eden

of comely splendour

let's ride on this chariot of bliss

to our royal castle of exotic delight

let the chamberlains roll out the red carpet

to welcome her royal princess

my elegant paragon of inestimable value

as we rekindle the flame of love

let the banquet begin...

LET LOVE...

This caste of ours
where gory tales
pervade with pride
and hapless wastrels
hobble the lanes
all conjure a picture of gloom!
they will cease with ease
if showers of love untainted
we express with glee
to those in need of one
this will keep our gladsome lives aglow
from the thorny pest of hate
for love has the power
to cover our world with radiance!
like the rose it blooms and blossoms
the fragrance like the myrtle lingers
like the gemstone it remains unblemished
like refined gold it glistens with resplendence
like the echoes of a pleasant song
it rings permanently in our hearts!
let's usher in the honey
to dine in our homes and domain
to heal scorched souls
to calm turbulent tides of torment
to ease the pain of puncture
like the crystal waters
that quench
the thirst of a yearning hiker
let love rule and reign
let love...

PRECIOUS PEARL

(For my cherished Princess Adetutu Onuchi-Mark)

You are an alluring specimen
whose charismatic gait of feline grace
exudes an aura of celestial glint
your elegance echoes a royal birthstone of grandeur
your intuitive candour surges rays of sunshine
your stately beauty of matchless inspiration
eloquently affirms your comeliness
of nubile ensemble
your exquisite gait like the gazelle
makes my heart ripple with ecstasy
your inner radiance epitomizes the strength of a godly character
pulsating with the glide of a conqueror
your svelte build of lovely perfection
complements your inner glow of unalloyed grace
a priceless treasure beyond measure
you have remained a firefly amidst night jars
the ilk of your breed remains a rare find
your nonpareil uniqueness epitomizes a stellar mould
- an extant breed bright as the morning rose
you are like the glow-worm whose graceful gait lightens darkened
paths
your seraphic gaze permeates this tainted orb with hope
your dulcet tone melodious like the canary
triggers all to intoxication like the new wine
behold your vestal bloom!
Sparkling like polished diamond
you speak with refreshing fire -
having drank from the gourd
of the custodian of wisdom
you are indeed well-groomed amazon
a maiden of idyllic haven
may you never cross the path of twilight hunters
may your very kind multiply and replenish the earth...

LIFE'S WARMTH

The warmth of life
like a flickering flame in winter
ignites the passion of attraction
in an orb of relentless chill
the warmth of life
like pelting flecks of frost in summer
inflames the ardour of appeal
in a globe of scorching blaze
enjoy the warmth of life
by being the warmth for searching hearts
be the flickering flame at dusk and in winter
be the pelting flecks of frost in summer
be the balm of laughter to frowning souls
and wailing hearts...
The radiance of your deeds
shall rise some day to dine with you
when you earnestly need it...
Karma never slumbers!

GENIAL PATH

I once trod this path

of sunshine's lonely glimpse

a habitation in vacuum

where I strolled with shadows

and staggered with scarecrows

a gangway of illusion

in search of a pathfinder of bliss

a journey through nature's bowel

without throwing in the towel

and a decision to bridge the chasm of gory erosion

in insulation, I searched with a flaming passion

until I met HIM!

The man who bore my pains

and took away my shame

by shedding his stainless blood

for a humanity that refused to acknowledge HIM

a surge of light engulfed my being

and I found meaning to my superficial sprint

in this restless maze of lingering mistiness

and murky memories

I found love...

My loneliness was gone...

Gone with the shadows of my hideous past

Doxology

AWESOME CREATOR

We sing your praise

with a thousand strings of endless delight

we marvel at your awe-inspiring magnificence

the aesthetics of your imaginative creation

splashed across the universe

with the celestial configuration of the moon, stars and sun

beyond the comprehension of your mortal vessels

your unquantifiable power is incontestable

we are a product of your artistic genius

let the harmony of your symphony

ring loud with blazing thunder!

PRICELESS ALLY

Your universal presence
has proved your essence
as a virtue of excellence
silently affirming your vocal eloquence
as an eternal gem of resplendence
exhibited by mortals through divine providence
for your crystal presence needs no evidence
though misinterpreted yet you still stand tall
because you conquer all
you are cherished by all
because you can never falter nor fall
you have transformed lives
even in strange territories your virtue thrives
you still soar amidst jibes and jives
because you are far from lust
empty of lethal crust
yours' an enduring quality
void of middle-of-the-road banality
specifically designed to serve humanity
let hate fizzle out and love reign
in our callous domain
so we can peace and joy maintain.

THE CROSS

For the callous heart of stone

His blood was shed to atone

for the sake of humanity He did bleed

and like a paschal lamb His vestal blood was shed

the path of sin through Him you must flee

by making a simple plea

to salvage you from transgression's cruel hold

so that you can join the heaven-bound fold

for the unrepentant plunderers and drainers of our wealth

who constantly sag the nation of its monetary health

shall be tossed into hell –

more fiery than an abandoned cell

...BEYOND DESCRIPTION

His awesome glory radiates with blissful splendour
beyond description is His lofty grandeur
His immeasurable love for mankind runs beyond the stretch of the Nile
making humanity have a cause to smile
His boundless wisdom outshines the depths of the Pacific
from the territory of the specific
to the sphere of the inexplicable
...He is always able!

From the peak of Everest to the lowest vale of convolution
His mighty arms are always available to lean on...
I'm proud to be a product of His celestial creation
an available vessel on a mission...
Driven by a passionate vision
because His inventive power is beyond comprehension
let every terrestrial creature pay obeisance...
To the One who rules and reigns!

...

The fireflies have come to nestle

upon the perching breathe of dawn

beyond foreboding dreams of dusk

a transit of dialogues...

Awaiting the drums

of rustling sunset...

The cycle rages on

CODA...

ABOUT THE AUTHOR

Onoruoiza Mark ONUCHI is a creative warhead, a Management and Corporate Communications Consultant. He is widely published in international anthologies and has been featured in The Guardian and ThisDay newspapers.